I0168892

O into L. Spadoni

Tombs and Catacombs of the Appian Way

(History of Cremation) a Lecture Delivered in Rome, January 1891...

Olinto L. Spadoni

Tombs and Catacombs of the Appian Way
(History of Cremation) a Lecture Delivered in Rome, January 1891...

ISBN/EAN: 9783337274979

Printed in Europe, USA, Canada, Australia, Japan

Cover: Foto ©ninafisch / pixelio.de

More available books at **www.hansebooks.com**

OLINTO L. SPADONI

TOMBS AND CATACOMBS

OF

THE APPIAN WAY.

✳✳

(History of Cremation)

A Lecture delivered in Rome, January 1891.

BEFORE A SELECT AUDIENCE OF ENGLISH AND AMERICAN VISITORS.

ROME

PRINTED BY THE SOCIETÀ LAZIALE

Piazza del Popolo, 8-14

—

1892

PRICE 50 CENTIMES.

Registered according to the Law of International Copyright. Translation Forbidden.

Ladies and Gentlemen,

The custom of burying the Dead together in a common and enclosed cemetery is not an ancient one.

During the most remote epochs in the history of man, that is during that long period which preceeded the establishment of different communities, each family had its own tomb within the limits of the family estate, which estate, besides the tomb, contained also the temple and the family residence.

The land which formed the estate was inalienable, and was tilled by the members of the family. They all lived together on it, and from it they derived their food. They prayed in the same temple to the same Gods, and when they died they were buried in the same tomb.

The State during these early periods of antiquity did not extend beyond the family boundary; and the father of each family was teacher, judge, master, priest, treasurer of his family or clan. When he died, his authority was transmitted to his eldest son.

With the gradual advance of civilization this patriarchal state of society suffered an evolution; prompted by the advantages which co-operation offered over isolation and competition, and for the sake of more effectual defence, families united together, and formed communities and cities. These cities were built, as far as it was practicable, in places near the lands possessed by the families who entered such unions; and then also arose the necessity of burying the Dead in a common burial-ground.

Thus, from the family tomb, existing within the limits of the family property during the patriarchal period, after the establishment of Communities, we come to the city cemetery. Now whether for the sake of public health, or for other reasons which we are unable to ascertain, the localities selected for burial were not within the city walls but outside them, along the public roads beyond the city gates.

Such was the case with the Pelasgian and Etruscans, as demonstrated by their cities and cemeteries. Such was the case with Rome, which was the highest expression of Etruscan civilization; and such was the case with all other cities, which derived from Rome.

During the dark and middle ages, when ancient culture and civilization were lost or slumbered under the thick strata of religious fanaticism and ignorance, the hygienic laws which had reached the highest degree in Rome were altogether lost sight of; and we find the Dead buried in the cloisters of convents in the crypts of churches or in the grave-yards adjoining churches.

Many a plague, during the middle ages, were caused by this promiscuity of the dead with the living.

In our present modern Italy a law was passed, which is an equivalent of the ancient Roman law of the twelve tables, prohibiting burials within the city limits; and every inhabitant, be he a layman or priest, prince, beggar, or Pope, must be buried outside the City walls.

As I have already stated, the public roads were the public cemeteries in ancient Rome. They were also selected by the people for their public walks and resorts, offering a greater attraction than the narrow streets of the city, on account of the monumental tombs and gardens which lined them, tombs and monuments, for the building and decoration of which the skill of the architect and painter was tasked, as well as that of the sculptor, mosaic maker and gardener. They were at times edifices of colossal dimensions, on whose decoration enormous sums of money were frequently lavished.

The noblest and wealthiest families had their mausoleums on the principal roads, along which property was more valuable than elsewhere. Poorer people had their tombs on roads of secondary importance.

In Rome the Via Latina and the Via Appia were amongst the most ancient roads and owing to the places to which they led as also to their antiquity, they were considered the most fashionable to be buried in. Here then, in preference to any other spot, the Roman aristocracy

at the time of the Republic, as well as the aristocracy of the Empire
buried their Dead. The Via Appia was the most important of all.
Its importance was such, that its fame passed to tradition, and spread
over the world. Even to-day the Via Appia is as well known as the
London Piccadilly, or the boulevards of Paris; and yet it dates back to
three thousand years.

It has been stated that the Via Appia was built by the Censor Appius
Claudius, the Blind, in the year 312, B. C. This statement is hardly
correct. Rome had roads connecting her with other cities, since the
time of her foundation.

We must say then, in order to be correct, that the Via Appia was
not *built* but *paved* by Appius, during his censorship of that year, as
Livy clearly states in the following words: " The censorship of Appius
Claudius and Caius Plautius of that year (442 A. U. C.) was famed,
and the name of Appius passed to posterity with greater celebrity for
having paved the Via Appia and brought to Rome a new supply of water."

From statements of Frontinus and of Livy, it is clear, a road existed
in that direction before the Appia. This road Appius restored, paved,
and reduced to military uses; and formed in a certain sense, a new
road to which he gave his name and which became in succession so
magnificent and celebrated, among the other Consular roads, that it was
called by Statius " Regina Viarum ", the Queen of roads.

The Via Appia began at the Porta Capena in the wall of Servius
Tullius. Remains of this gate exist even to-day under the Osteria of
that name, which is about three or four hundred yards beyond the
Church of St. Gregory the Great.

The part paved by Appius extended forty miles beyond the Capena
gate. At that point one of the *mutationes*, or stations, was established;
which was named also, after the Censor; Appii Forum.

The road was paved as far as Appii Forum, and was extended by the
same Censor unpaved as far as Capua, near Naples. Later on the Via Appia,
from Capua, was extended to Beneventum and Brundusium, becoming
thus the principal connecting thoroughfare between Rome and the far
East. The width of the road varied, at different points, between 11 and 14
Roman feet. Consequently, even in its narrowest parts it was sufficiently wide to allow two chariots to drive abreast; the width of Roman
chariots and cars, never exceeded five Roman feet from wheel to wheel.

Each mile of the road was marked by stone or marble pillars. A number of them have been discovered, and the inscriptions, engraved upon them, show that the road was restored by Vespasian, Domitian, Nerva, Trajan, Septimius Severus, Caracalla and Diocletian.

On the balustrade of the Capitoline hill, near the colossal groups of Castor and Pollux, are to be seen two of these mile-stones of the Appia. They belong to the restoration of Septimius Severus, and they marked the ends of the first and seventh mile of that road.

The first of these has a special importance. There had been a controversy between archaeologists as to whether the roads, which issued from the city, were measured from the golden mile-stone, placed in the Roman Forum by Caesar Augustus, or from their respective gates.

The pillar in question was found in 1520 in a vineyard along the Appia, where the road is now crossed by the railway line to Pisa. In 1867 Professor Parker, the eminent English archaeologist, measured one thousand paces, 1618 English yards, corresponding to a Roman mile, from the spot where the pillar was found, in the direction of Rome. At the end of the thousand paces he excavated, and discovered the remains of the square towers which flanked the Porta Capena already mentioned and from which the road evidently started. His discovery settled the disputed point in favour of those, who sustained that the roads were measured from the city gates.

But although the measurements of Roman roads did not commence in the Roman Forum, the gilt pillar af Augustus, the *milliarium aureum*, was none the less the point at which all roads joined; the *umbilicus*, or the centre of the city, being near it.

Every Roman city had a central mark to which all roads of the province converged, and the London stone is supposed to be the centre of the Roman roads of ancient Britain.

The Consular roads had *mutationes*, or stations, at intervals of ten miles, at which stations travellers changed horses. The postal arrangements belonged to the executive, and were established for the use of magistrates and officers travelling on official duty. Private people could not use the Roman post, and were obliged to provide their own conveyances. The average rate of travelling over the Roman roads, by post, was ten miles per hour in the plain; but less on hilly regions. The first *mutationes* of the Appia from Rome were: Bovillae, at a distance of ten miles, Sublanuvium at twenty, Sponsas at thirty, and Appii Forum at forty miles.

Three miles beyond the *mutatio* of Sublanuvium, was another *mutatio;* but this had no reference whatever to the postal arrangement of the Appia, though it stood on it. This *mutatio* was called: *ad tres tabernas,* and, as together with Appii Forum this station is mentioned in the Acts of the Apostles in reference to St. Paul's journey to Rome, I must explain the reason why this *mutatio* stood on the Appia, though it was not used for service of that road, and its vicinity, only three miles, to the preceeding station of Sublanuvium.

At *Tres Tabernas,* namely at a distance of 23 miles from Rome, the Via Appia was crossed by a road which came from Antium, on the sea coast, and continued in the direction of Velitrae till it reached the Via Latina beyond.

The *mutatio* called ad *Tres Tabernas* was the one established at the point where this Antium road crossed the Appia; but it was for service of the postal arrangements of the road which led from Antium to Velitrae and the Via Latina, and not of the Appia, as already stated.

Immediately outside the Porta Capena, on the left, was the monument and tomb of Horatia, the unfortunate sister of the Roman champion whose valour, against the Curiatii brothers of Alba, insured the liberty and the very existence of Rome. The tomb of Horatia was on the exact spot where she fell, murdered by Horatio, when on his triumphal return to the city, he was met there by his sister who reproached him the successes over the Curiatii, on the plea that one of them was betrothed to her. No remains exist of the monument in question.

Beyond the tomb of Horatia, on the right-hand side of the Appia, where the Church of the St. Nereus and Achilleus now stands, the celebrated Temple of Mars once stood.

From this temple, on the 15th. of June of each year the Cavalry or Equestrian order started at full gallop and entered the city gate whence they proceeded to the Capitol. This charge was made by five thousand knights, in commemoration of the celebrated cavalry charge, by which the victory of lake Regillus was assured to the

Romans with liberty to the republic. The cavalry entered the Capena at full speed, and continued so through the whole length of the Via Triumphalis, as far as the *Meta Sudans* near the Colosseum. At this point, where the Via Sacra began, the knights slackened their pace and proceeded at a walking pace towards the temple of Castor and Pollux in the Roman Forum, erected there in commemoration of the lake Regillus' victory. The Censor, from the prominent podium of this temple, reviewed the cavalry, as they, palm in hand, solemnly and martially proceeded along towards the Capitol, where on the ara, in front of the temple of Jupiter, they offered sacrifices and returned thanksgivings to that deity.

Beyond the church of the St. Nereus and Achilleus, on the left, the celebrated Via Latina branched off from the Appia. The ruin of a shrine marks the deviation of that road.

Still further, beyond the church of St. Caesareus, which stands on the site of the temple of Tempest, in the year 1780 the tomb of the Scipiones was discovered. This monument has the greatest importance for history and ancient topography, as well as for conveying the idea of the state of art in Rome during the fifth century after her foundation. Cicero in his Tusculan Disputations mentions this tomb as immediately outside the Porta Capena and as near the monuments of the Colatinii, Servilii, and Metelli. Of these, only the tomb of the Scipiones has come to light.

Before reaching the so-called arch of Drusus and the porta St. Sebastiano, is the well known Villa Condini. In these orchards, in the year 1822, were discovered three columbaria belonging to the Caesars, and in which were buried the servants of the Palatine hill. Inscriptions found in these burial places show them as having been in use from the end of the republic up to the time of the Emperor Nero, 69. A. D. It was under this Emperor that Triphena and Triphosa, two slaves or servants belonging to the household of the Caesar, died on the Palatine. Alike their fellow-servants they were buried in the Imperial Columbaria, as testified by the marble tablets which were discovered there *in situ*, in 1822.

The interest afforded by a visit to these columbaria, could not be greater for Christians, when we consider that we have here the ashes of these members of the Imperial household who were Christians in

Rome, only about 40 years after the death of Christ. Triphena and Triphosa are mentioned by St. Paul in his letters to the Romans and Colossians.

Proceeding, after the Porta St. Sebastiano, along this road as far as Albano, we find more ruins of tombs, villas, and temples; so many brick, stone, and marble witnesses of the ancient grandeur of the " Queen of Roads ".

Our object here is not to guide the visitor to recognise each particular ruin. That can only be done on the spot. But for the benefit of those among you who have not accompanied me on that important excursion, I will make the best of it, and try to explain as much about it, as possible. If we do not succeed in forming an accurate idea of the whole, we shall obtain an approximate one; and that will be better than nothing.

The Appia road from the Porta St. Sebastiano to Albano is a straight one. Among the principal objects of interest we meet on the road at this distance of 13 miles, are the tomb of Geta, the murdered brother of Caracalla, and the church of *Domine quo vadis*, supposed to be the spot where the Saviour appeared to St. Peter when that Apostle was leaving the city so as to escape the Neronian persecution.

Then other columbariums, and the intricate labyrinth of the Catacombs of St. Sebastian and St. Callixtus; then the well preserved Circus of Romulus the son of Maxentius, built near Romulus' tomb by his father Maxentius, in order to celebrate the games, which he had instituted at the death of his son, as if he had been a God; then we see the mighty fortress-like tomb of Cecilia Metella " the wealthiest Roman's wife "; the tomb of Seneca, the philosopher of Cordoba victim of his pupil the Emperor Nero; the tomb of the Pompeii; the tomb of Usia, the priestess of Isis; the battle-field where the Curiatii and the Horatii fought for the preservation of the liberty of their respective cities, and the tombs erected on the spot where they fell, the Villa of the Quintilii, those just brothers, who in the corrupted times in which they lived paid with their lives their riches and their virtues; the tombs of Cotta, the Consul, of Severus and Galienus; the Villa and spot where Clodius fell by Milo's dagger, and lastly, just in front of the city gate of Albano, the colossal mausoleum in which the Great Pompeius deposited the remains of Giulia, Caesars' daughter, his first wife, and where he himself was afterwards buried by Cornelia, his second wife.

A sad spectacle is offered to-day by the tomb of the great Roman, who found Asia Minor the boundary of the Empire and left it its centre. To-day, chickens and hens sing a constant and not harmonious concert in that funereal chamber, where the ashes of the hero would have rested peacefully, had it not been for the spoliation of man. Instead of this, the rooster erects his proud head, and holds sway there, in and over this tomb...... and the dung hill near.

Having given you an idea of the road, we must turn now to study one of its principal attractions, the catacombs.

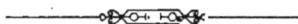

We have had in Italy, during antiquity, three distinct religious epochs. The very first religion the Italians had, was the religion of their fathers or the worship of their ancestors.

After death, every man was considered as a God. The most respectful epithets they could think of, were bestowed upon the dead by the living. They were called good, holy, and happy. The living entertained for the dead all the veneration man could have for a God whom they loved and feared.

This apotheosis was not merely the privilege of great men; but every man, after death, was entitled to the veneration of his posterity, even if during his lifetime his life had been the reverse of virtuous and honourable. — Sinful men became Gods as well as good men; the only difference being, that the virtuous continued to be virtuous after death and the wicked retained their wickedness for all Eternity.

It is positive; as too many proofs have attested, that during the very earliest epochs, when the only religious sentiment Italians had, consisted in the worship of their dead, corpses were embalmed and buried.

The production of telluric motions and volcanism, in this land of fire, as Italy has been so appropriately called, and the fright they exercised upon the people, were considered as holy punishments sent by the *Dead* for the faults committed by their posterity. It was customary then, to propitiate the good-will of the Dead by sacrifices. When these cataclisms appeared and were considered as the tangible manifestations of the wrath of the departed ones, the terror and panic-striken people gave themselves up to all sorts of propitiations and sacrifices so as to appease their angry ancestral deities and thus end their terrible vengeance. As fire was the predominating element of these telluric commotions, that never previously seen element was considered as a living and huge monster exacting thousands and thousands of animal and human victims; a monster who raged ewerywhere, multiplying itself everywhere, and which neither man nor thing could resist. A monster, who scorched those he approached, and who brought desolation and death wherever he appeared.

The poet Lucretus in his masterly work on the "Nature of the Universe," says: "and all mortals are so thoroughly overcome by fright, when they witness so many phenomena in Heaven and Earth, which they cannot understand, that they think everything happens by Divine will."

Thus fire, the principal protagonist of volcanism and of the explosions of nature, was considered at first as the agent by which their ancestors and Gods, punished posterity for faults committed. Then, owing firstly to its own monstruosity, when its usefullness became known it was venerated as a new religion, the religion of nature's forces; nature in her good and evil influences.

Hence we have two religions; not one against the other, but rather completing themselves. The one, the worship of fire, was the adoration of nature; the second, the adoration of human soul. — Consequently, on this religious innovation, the way by which bodies were disposed of, after death, underwent a change; entombment was replaced by cremation.

By cremation, the elements forming the two religions could not complete each other in a more effectual way; as men, at the moment of their death, namely when they became Gods, received, by that, the consecration of that other religious power; "fire." — Thus the apotheosis meant, not only the passage of man to the state of a deity, but the real transformation and absorbtion of corpses by the Deity Fire.

Cremation, as far as it can be ascertained, prevailed in Italy during the patriarchal period; that is before the establishment of communities.

When cities were founded, cremation ceased generally, if not altogether.

Saturn is supposed, and seems, to have been the pioneer of city founders; for, if tradition is correct, he was the first to give abode to his people in the city which was called Saturnia after him. The Capitol is the site of ancient Saturnia.

For the sake of conciseness, and as the subject of this lecture does not call for it, I cannot devote now more time to Saturn and his times. Suffice it to say, that the hero was killed by the Iberians when they invaded Italy and assailed and took the Capitol. The inhabitants of Saturnia, not able to hold out, gave themselves to flight. There was no time for them to pay their chief and benefactor, the funeral honours due him and much less was there time to cremate his body; so it is supposed that Saturn's corpse was hurriedly buried by his people on the southern slope of the Saturnian hill, while probably the Iberians were scaling the city from the opposite side.

There, the body lay, for a considerable lapse of time, without ever receiving the tribute due to the Dead by their posterity, until the fortunes of the Italians being retrieved having re-taken possession of their territory and of the Saturnian city, they were able at last to accomplish his funeral.

Their first thought soon after their victories was to uncover Saturn's grave and pay him, tenfold, those divine honours, which circumstances and danger had prevented them from rendering at the time of his death. The Saturnalian festivals in Rome, were the annual repetition of the funeral ceremony held at the grave of the hero on the slope of the Capitol, where the ruins of his temple are still to be seen.

Circumstances had rendered necessary the burial of Saturn instead of his cremation. The fact that this pioneer of civilization was buried, instead of being cremated as customary, brought about a change in the way of disposing of the Dead in Rome. Cremation was then abandoned and burial adopted.

Burials lasted for the whole of the kingly period, and for the greater part of the time of Republic that followed.

In 78 B. C. Sylla, the dictator, died at Puteoli. His body was brought to Rome in a golden litter and a funeral, worthy a king's, was celebrated in the Campus Martius, not far from where we are now assembled. Here his body was cremated, and cremated in fulfilment of his express will, and by order of his relations. Historians state that Sylla wished to be cremated, according to the ancient custom, so that his corpse might not meet the fate of his antagonist's, Caius Marius, who was disinterred by his order, and after having been dragged through the streets, was thrown in the river Anio, as the corpse of a parricide.

From the example thus set by Sylla, the chief of the aristocratic party, cremation became again the fashion among the nobles, and few years later, it became generally adopted. During the whole time of the Empire, burial was seldom, if ever practised.

The Hebrews seem to have always adhered to the system of burial and to have discarded cremation altogether. Thus Christ, according to the Jewish custom, was buried.

With the introduction and propagation of Cristianity in Rome, the adherents to the new religion, in veneration to the Founder of their Faith again adopted burial, and after the complete triumph of the Church, cremation was again completely abandoned in the Roman Empire.

To-day cremation is reviving in Italy, and in almost every cemetery of our large cities, appropriate crematories have been established. It is curious to note that this revival of cremation in our country should have had for pioneer a child of Albion, Shelley the poet, whose body was cremated on the sea shore near Viareggio, by his friend Byron.

These observations on the history of cremation in Rome were rendered necessary for explaining the origin of the Catacombs.

Thus, resuming, we have three distinct epochs in Italy when burial prevails: The first, during the patriarchal state of the people, preceeding the establishment of the worship of Fire; The second, from Saturn to Sylla, that is during the whole of the Roman epoch until 70 B. C.; the third, from the introduction of Christianity to the present day, when, as everything tends to show, cremation will probably again become general.

The tombs of the Via Appia, as already observed, belonged to the most ancient, and therefore to the noblest of Roman families.

During the Empire, when by the conquests of Rome the riches of the whole world were collected here, all the temples, palaces, and tombs, were rebuilt in costly materials; But the sites of the temples, palaces and tombs remained the original ones.

Before proceeding further to the explanation of the Catacombs, it is necessary to say how the Roman family was constituted.

The Roman family, or *gens,* was constituted on a totally different basis from that upon which the family is established at present.

The Roman family preserved during the whole of the Roman epoch considerable remnants of the institutions by which families were governed during the ancient patriarchal time. The family was a regular clan, a complete institution within itself, held by a special religion and governed by special laws; and its members were numbered by hundreds, sometimes by thousands. The Roman *gens,* or family, celebrated the same sacred ceremonies, foremost among which, being the adoration of the *Dii Gentiles,* Gods who protected, and were invoked by the *gens* only.

The whole *gens* answered for the debts of its members, redeemed their prisoners, paid the fines of their condemned. If a member of a *gens* became magistrate, each member of the clan paid a share towards defraying the expenses of keeping him in office; and the accused was accompanied in front of the tribunal by all the members of his *gens,* as a token of the solidarity extant between the members and the body to which they belonged.

We must make a distinction between the *gens,* and the family; as the word family has to-day quite a different meaning from the one it had during antiquity. *Gens* is the name which corresponds to the modern meaning of *clan*; whereas the Roman word *familia* meant, in its widest significance, the totality of that which belonged to a Roman citizen who was a *paterfamilias.*

Thus in certain cases of testamentary disposition the word *familia* is explained by the equivalent, *patrimonium,* patrimony. Thus *familia* was the estate or patrimony held by a *paterfamilias* and received by him in inheritance from his ancestors, and which he was obliged to transmit intact to posterity. Hence *paterfamilias* meant father or chief, or master, or administrator of the estate, goods chattels and cattle belonging to a *gens,* or clan. By the laws which governed the *gens,* the *paterfamilias* was jointly their chief, treasurer, judge, priest, and military leader. In very ancient times he had the right of life and death over all. When the Sabine *gens* of the Claudii came to settle in Rome, the three thousand persons composing it, obeyed only one chief. When the Fabii *gens* took upon themselves the task of carrying on the war against Veii we find they had a chief, who spoke in their name before the Senate and the same chief led them against the enemy.

The *gens*, however, was not associations of families, but a large family. In fact even philologically *gens* stands for *genus* both corresponding to the verb *gignere*, to the substantive *genitor*, words implying all the idea of progeny, and continuity. Each *gens* having originated from a common stock, they venerated the same deified ancestor; and their offerings and sacrifices were always deposited upon an altar, which was always the tomb of the venerated ancestor and founder of the *gens*. As the *gens* resided on the same estate, as they had a common ancestor, as they worshipped the same gods, as they helped each other, as they were mutually responsible of all their actions, as they formed a total whole, so were they also buried together in a common sepulchre.

Clients and slaves forming as they did part of a *gens*, were also buried in the same tomb. The reciprocal need which the rich had of the poor, and the poor of the rich, made servants. During the patriarchal state servant and slave were synonimous. The domestic religion did not allow of admitting a stranger into the family; it was thus necessary to find some means, by which to make a strange servant a member and an integral part of the family. That was done by initiating the new comer to the family worship; and the initiation consisted in bringing the slave in front of the household fire, and there in presence of the Lares, the paterfamilias poured pure water over the head of the slave. The ceremony ended by a banquet consisting of cakes of pure wheat, fruits, and wine shared between the members of the family and the newly admitted slave.

The meaning of this ceremony was that the newly come, hitherto a stranger, became a member of the family, having acquired its religion by the consecration and banquet which had taken place in honour of, and shared also by the family Lares. From that moment the slave took part in the family prayers and the family festivals; the household fire protected him, and the religion and the protection of the Lares belonged equally to him as they did to his master. For the said reasons THE SLAVE WAS NECESSARILY BURIED IN THE SAME FAMILY SEPULCHRE.

The right which the servant acquired of worshipping and praying with the rest of the family, deprived him of his liberty. Religion was a bond which kept him chained to that family for his whole life,. and for all the time which followed his death.

Though his master could raise him from his servile state and make him a free man, still the servant could not leave the family in which he had entered by sacred rituals. As religion had made him a member of the family, he could not separate himself from it without committing a sacrilegious act and thus incur the wrath and the vengeance of the Gods. Liberated servants continued to recognise the authority of the chief, or patron, or father of the family not only, but if they married, their children had to do the same; as no marriage was possible without the permission of the patron. Marriage was impossible without the consent of the patron, because hymen was a religious family ceremony which, as such, was performed by the patron, or father, the high priest of his own family worship.

Thus a number of small families were constituted in the bosom of the patron's family, who with its direct and collateral branches, its servants or slaves, and its liberated slaves, or clients, united, formed a group of men numbering hundreds and thousands of persons, all residing together, if not on the same estate, on the property belonging to the same master or patron for their life-time; and were all buried together in the same family tomb after death.

By law, if a patron had no children to whom to leave his patrimony, he was required to adopt one of his near relatives thus insuring the continuity of the family, with the constant worshippers to the Gods of the *gens*. Therefore, as tombs were inviolable, for they contained the bodies of the deified ancestors, and consequently inalienable, they required to be extensive places, sufficiently large enough to give shelter to the dead of a whole *gens*, whose members numbered thousands; and this not for a generation but for all times to come.

———— ∘✦⊙┥ ┝⊙✦∘ ————

As I have already noted, the tombs of the Via Appia, as well as those which lined other roads issuing from Rome, were rebuilt during

the Empire with more costly materials, but the sites of the tombs
rebuilt remained the same.

A Roman family tomb, especially during the Republic when, you
must remember Ladies and Gentlemen, the Dead were buried and not
cremated, was required to be necessarily of very extensive dimensions
so as to furnish accomodation for all the Dead of a family.

Land on the Via Appia was very valuable, and the Roman paterfamilias could not make a compromise by burying his direct and nearest
relatives in the family tomb of the Via Appia and his clients and slaves
elsewhere where land was not so valuable.

We have seen that all members of a *gens* were required to be buried
together in their sepulchre; therefore to do otherwise would have been
sacrilegious.

The problem of burying so many people in one sepulchre was solved
by the Romans in a very simple way. They took advantage of the
compact formation of the sandy soil of the Roman Campagna. Suppose
a field owned by a *gens* for the purpose of burial along the Via Appia;
in this field was erected the stone mausoleum capable of containing
a large number of sarchopaghi, in which which were placed the
bodies of those belonging to the direct lineage of the family proper;
at the back of the mausoleum was the forum or open space where
the funeral orations in honour of the Dead were delivered, and where
the funeral banquets were held; and also where the gladiatorial fights
and other games were given.

Around the monument, the open area, and the other places adjoining the tomb, was a railing or a small ditch marked by boundary stones; which ditch formed the sacred limits of the abode of the
Dead, which no one could trespass. In a word, it was a proper *pomerium*,
similar to the one which surrounded as a sacred boundary of City.

Below the surface, in narrow passages excavated in tufa, loculi or
niches were cut right and left for the reception of the bodies of the
less important members of the *gens*, namely the clients and slaves. Steps
led from the interior of the funeral chamber of the mausoleum where
the sarcophaghi were, down to the crypt; so that all those underground passages were nothing else but the supplement of the funeral
chamber above.

These underground passages could not be excavated beyond the limits of the area above ground, as that would have been trespassing over the soil belonging to the tomb of a neighbouring *gens*. But by turnings, and by making the passages parallel, and by extending these passages to the same length as the area above, an infinite number of niches for depositing the dead could be obtained. For these passages were sufficiently deep, as to allow, in some cases, even twelve niches to be cut in them one above the other.

The niches were deep enough to allow from one to four bodies being placed in them. When the niches on the level of this first flooring had all been filled, a second excavation was made, and an additional series of passages were cut below the original one, and another stairway placed them in communication, the upper with the lower one. In many cases, when the family had large numbers of clients and slaves, these crypts were four, five, and even more stories deep.

The introduction of cremation, commencing as we have seen with Sylla, in 78 B. C., put an end to the custom of burying in these underground passages. It is worthy of note, that when this occurred, the bonds of religion had already been considerably slackened. The epoch of Caesar Augustus was prominently an epoch of unbelief and atheism; and although that Emperor did all in his power to restore the ancient credit of the Gods of the Roman Olympus, the masses, and especially the wealthier and more cultivated people became more sceptical than ever, and the once venerated Gods became frequently the subject of satirical jokes and sarcasms. Consequently, during the Empire, owing to the revival of cremation, and owing to the discredit in which Gods and religion had fallen, it was possible to accomplish with impunity that which three, or even two hundred years before, would have been considered as the greatest crime committed against all human and divine laws, I mean the burial of clients and slaves and even relatives, away from the tomb of their ancestors and patrons.

Already towards the latter end of the Republic, there were separate *columbaria* for the servants and clients of the nobles. With the Empire, the Caesars built others for depositing there the ashes of the members of their households; and even enterprisers were not wanting, who built *columbaria* with the object of speculation by allowing the ashes of the dead to be deposited in them, on payment of a sum of money.

It is needless for me to explain what the *columbaria* were, and how they were built. There are so many preserved in Rome, that every one of you will have seen some.

———————•⊙⟨⊙⟩⊙⟨⊙⟩⊙•———————

Thus from the year 78 B. C. the crypts for slaves and clients, under the gorgeous mausoleums of the patricians of the Via Appia and other roads, commenced to be abandoned; and remained so, until they were used again by the Christians, that is, for over a century and a half.

———————•⊙⟨⊙⟩⊙⟨⊙⟩•———————

Christianity as you well know, Ladies and Gentlemen, found its first and warmest adherents in Rome, among the higher classes. By degrees, and specially after the end of the first century, family after family embraced the new faith.

As already stated during this, I fear, too long discourse, in homage to the way in which the body of Christ had been disposed after his crucifixion, the pagan converts to Christianity again discarded cremation and re-adopted burial.

The noble Christian ladies of Rome and their families then buried their relatives and their kindred in their ancient mausoleums and in the crypts extant below them. The crypt of one family was later, placed in communication with the crypt of that of a neighbour and thus catacombs were formed. I use the word catacombs with the significance of " general, early Christians, cemeteries ", the ethymology of the word proper meaning underground tomb, or excavation, or subterranean place; the first to be called so being the one in which the bodies of Peter and Paul were deposited at the Cemetery of St. Sebastian.

Evidently, when the ancient pagan loculi became occupied by the Christians, the remains of those originally deposited there, had to be removed, in order to make room for the bodies of the brethren of the new faith

———————•⊙⟨⊙⟩⊙⟩•———————

I would like to continue, and lay before you other uncontestable arguments, demonstrating that the Catacombs are not, in a general way, the work of the Christians; but as the demonstration would require considerable time, I cannot inflict it on you at the present moment. That will probably form the subject of another lecture, if you have not found me too tedious; which I hope to have the honour of delivering before some of you at least, if your kindness and your patronage may continue to be bestowed upon your grateful, but unworthy servant.

www.ingramcontent.com/pod-product-compliance
Lightning Source LLC
Chambersburg PA
CBHW031158090426
42738CB00008B/1388